ISEAS
at 50

ISEAS
at 50

Understanding Southeast Asia
Past and Present

by
Prime Minister Lee Hsien Loong,
Professor Wang Gungwu
and
Professor Leonard Y. Andaya

ISEAS YUSOF ISHAK
INSTITUTE

Published in Singapore in 2018 by
ISEAS Publishing
30 Heng Mui Keng Terrace
Singapore 119614
E-mail: publish@iseas.edu.sg
Website: <http://bookshop.iseas.edu.sg>

The responsibility for facts and opinions in this publication rests exclusively with the authors and their interpretations do not necessarily reflect the views or the policy of the publisher or its supporters.

ISEAS Library Cataloguing-in-Publication Data

Lee, Hsien Loong.
    ISEAS at 50 : Understanding Southeast Asia Past and Present / Lee Hsien Loong, Wang Gungwu and Leonard Y. Andaya.
    1. Southeast Asia—Study and teaching—History.
    2. Southeast Asia—Study and teaching—Singapore—History.
    3. ISEAS – Yusof Ishak Institute—History.
    I. Wang, Gungwu, 1930–
    II. Andaya, Leonard Yuzon, 1942–
DS524.8 S6L471   2018

ISBN 978-981-4818-99-5 (hard cover)
ISBN 978-981-4843-00-3 (ebook, PDF)

Typeset by Superskill Graphics Pte Ltd
Printed in Singapore by Markono Print Media Pte Ltd

Contents

Introduction

Mr Choi Shing Kwok
Director, ISEAS – Yusof Ishak Institute

It gives us great pleasure to present to you three public lectures given to commemorate ISEAS – Yusof Ishak Institute's 50th Anniversary. Much thought was invested in the decision to mark our anniversary with public lectures. Instead of celebrating the occasion with a grand gala dinner as is the norm, we decided on public lectures because they reflect more meaningfully our broader intellectual mission, namely, to provide expert knowledge on Southeast Asia to the informed public.

The first public lecture was delivered by Professor Leonard Y. Andaya entitled "Developments in the Scholarship of Southeast Asian Studies" on 21 February 2018 at the Institute. We invited Professor Andaya to speak on the state of Southeast Asian Studies because it is important for a research centre to continuously take stock of its core activity. Professor Andaya charted the ups and downs of Southeast Asian Studies from the 1960s to the present. He began with the early works of scholars like O.W. Wolters and Harry Benda (ISEAS's first Director) who wanted to bring to fore the stories of local communities. This was partly driven by the desire to give voice to these communities and partly by the need to understand the behaviour, practices and habits of local people as the Vietnam War raged on. Interest in Southeast Asian Studies declined in the United States after the end

1

of the Vietnam War. Many universities saw budget cuts and fewer PhDs were churned out.

There was a slight upswing in interest in the 1980s as children of migrants from Southeast Asia to the United States wanted to learn about the cultures and languages of their parents. By the 1990s, Professor Andaya noted that there were intense debates over the usefulness of area studies and if they should give way to traditional disciplines like anthropology and sociology. The 11 September 2001 attacks in the United States was another pivotal moment which saw a deft diversion of funds towards the study of the Middle East and South Asia because of their large Muslim populations. Professor Andaya also brought up the perennial question of English as the language of publication. The dominance of English as the preferred language for publication and, subsequently, peer recognition, came at the expense of publications in the respective vernacular languages of the region.

Professor Andaya also made a case for an "open system" of enquiry into Southeast Asia. By this he meant that the boundaries of scholarship should not be limited to artificial borders "whether constructed by governments, international organisation, or academic bodies — but by subject matter". In other words, a thematic and helicopter approach to issues is preferred. Finally, he noted that much of Southeast Asian Studies today is driven by "presentism bias", that is, research that is highly relevant to present-day concerns or subjects that are in demand by the job market. He urged that this should not come at the expense of textual and literary studies of the region.

The second public lecture was delivered by Prime Minister (PM) Lee Hsien Loong on 13 March 2018 at the Orchard Hotel. PM Lee had also delivered the keynote address at ISEAS's 25th Anniversary in 1993 while he was Deputy Prime Minister, and it was thus fitting that he would do us the honour again on the Institute's 50th birthday. PM Lee's public lecture was accompanied by a public exhibition that illustrated ISEAS's history, work and people. The exhibition provided the audience with an overview of ISEAS's humble beginnings on Bukit Timah campus in 1968 to its present-day location at Heng Mui Keng Terrace. They also laid out the evolving research agenda through the decades as well as the Institute's more recent archaeological endeavours in Singapore.

PM Lee's lecture began by making clear ISEAS's *raison d'être*. The 1960s was a tumultuous time in the region marked by the Vietnam War, *Konfrontasi* between Malaysia and Indonesia, and communist insurgencies in Thailand, Malaysia and Singapore. Singapore's independence in 1965 came with its own set of domestic challenges such as unemployment, the need for mass housing, and a stagnant economy. Yet despite these urgent challenges, PM Lee observed that "Our founding fathers were acutely conscious that to survive in a difficult environment, a small and newly independent country needed to acquire a deep understanding of the region. Because small countries do not shape world events, events shape us." Singapore had to quickly acquire, in Dr Goh Keng Swee's words, "a delicacy of perception" of complex regional affairs in order to foresee difficulties and opportunities. In other words, understanding the region was just as important as the pressing domestic challenges of the newly independent city-state. ISEAS was thus established.

With Singapore serving as the Association of Southeast Asian Nations (ASEAN) Chair for 2018, PM Lee went on to speak of the historical and contemporary importance of the grouping. He noted that ASEAN's original objective was political as the five founding members needed a regional platform for dialogue and co-operation. Through the decades, ASEAN had succeeded in forming a strong consensus for the international rule of law, the inviolability of international borders, and the legitimacy of national governments. It had also succeeded in economic co-operation in the later years. Today, the ASEAN Economic Community is a diverse yet dynamic grouping of ten member states with a growing population of 630 million. It is also a young population where 60 per cent are under 30 years of age. ASEAN could expect to form the fourth largest single market by 2030, after the United States, China and the EU.

Nevertheless, PM Lee flagged several challenges. ASEAN does not have a unified strategic outlook. One example of this is the lack of common ground over the South China Sea issue. Even the four claimant states — Vietnam, Malaysia, Brunei and the Philippines — have different attitudes on the issue. In short, ASEAN needs to maintain a coherent institutional identity while accommodating diverse national interests. PM Lee concluded by returning to the need for ISEAS to understand all these regional dynamics and to develop a "delicacy of perception" for the benefit of its stakeholders.

The third and final public lecture was delivered by Professor Wang Gungwu, the Chairman of the Institute's Board of Trustees. His lecture was titled "Before Southeast Asia: Passages and Terrains" and was held at the Orchard Hotel on 3 October 2018. While Professor Andaya's lecture dwelt on how Southeast Asia was studied through the decades, Professor Wang asked the more fundamental question — what was Southeast Asia?

Professor Wang began by observing that prior to the sixteenth century, the region was characterized by diversity of people scattered across the lands. They were too fragmented to form a political entity. Instead they were open to new ideas and goods, and were able to pick and choose practices and values to adopt, or what scholars called "local genius". Local genius allowed many Southeast Asian communities to reconcile indigenous features with political and religious practices imported from China or India. As such, there was no compelling need for these communities to form a region. After the sixteenth century, Professor Wang argued that it became "convenient" for external powers to see Southeast Asia as a region. The earlier Mongol expansion into China led to migration down from north Asia, thus creating a border between China and what laid below. Politics in Europe also began to have an impact in the region with the Spaniards taking over the Philippines, resulting in the latter's outlier status for a long time.

The eighteenth century ushered in industrial and scientific revolutions in Europe. They consequently shaped Southeast Asia more sharply. European powers in the form of colonialism marked out borders more definitively. The naval dominance of colonial powers led to the dominance of inlands. Colonial ports gave way to colonial states, thus introducing new political entities to indigenous peoples.

By the twentieth century land borders across Southeast Asia were firm. Nevertheless, the Japanese invasion of the region and the response to this invasion from 1941 to 1945 were the most defining events in the shaping of Southeast Asia. Another key period for the region were the years between 1963 and 1967. They were crucial to the emergence of ASEAN in 1967, itself a product of the Cold War. The fear of communism and the "domino effect" theory helped coalesce the five founding member states. By the 1990s, ASEAN-5 became ASEAN-10. During this time, the grouping faced a new geopolitical landscape and challenges like globalization. Regionalism was in full swing and yet many member states continued to be preoccupied with their own national development and priorities built on colonial legacies and borders. In effect, national forces were creating tension with regionalism, thus producing contradictions that ASEAN had to grapple with.

Professor Wang concluded his public lecture by opining that while it was always good for ASEAN to speak with one voice, this should not be pushed too fast given the tension above. Furthermore, he mused that different external powers were keen on ASEAN speaking with one voice but only if this voice was united on its side. More importantly, the region needed to retain its history of openness. The ability of Southeast Asian communities to choose and adapt external ideas and practices, while retaining local characteristics was a strength and not a weakness. And it was this ability that would allow the region to remain plugged into the rest of the world while preserving its autonomy.

Collectively, these three public lectures have exhorted ISEAS to continuously reflect on its research agenda, the region, as well as the contemporary landscape and challenges it has to operate in. They illustrate vividly how interest in Southeast Asian Studies waxed and waned over decades according to geopolitical concerns, especially from the United States; and more crucially, as a small country, how Singapore cannot afford to ignore or marginalize Southeast Asian research because our understanding of the region is crucial to our survival. We would do well to support Southeast Asian research regardless of trends elsewhere.

My thanks to Tan Chin Tiong, former Director of ISEAS and now Senior Advisor, who helped initiate these lectures. I hope you enjoy them as much as we enjoyed bringing them to you.

50th Anniversary Public Lecture

by

Professor Leonard Y. Andaya

on

21 February 2018
3.00 p.m. to 4.30 p.m.
ISEAS – Yusof Ishak Institute

Opening Remarks

Professor Wang Gungwu
Chairman, ISEAS Board of Trustees

I have two happy duties to perform today. The first is to open the celebration for the 50th Anniversary of the ISEAS – Yusof Ishak Institute. I am delighted to be here to celebrate this occasion fifty years after its establishment. The institute has certainly had its memorable moments during its exciting journey through the years.

I have had the privilege of following the institute's life from its beginnings and often wondered how it would fare given the extraordinary circumstances of Southeast Asia when Dr Goh Keng Swee came up with his idea of an institute. As I recall, he was not sure how it would develop, but had looked at several possible models. Dr Goh was very wise. He soon focused on some of the major universities that had institutes or centres of Southeast Asian Studies, in particular, Cornell University and Monash University. The former was already established and famous while the other was new. They both gave him valuable ideas as to how to plan his new institute.

He had a research-oriented model in mind but the practical side of it was always to help the people in Singapore to understand the region. It is easy now to forget that the regional leaders and officials responsible for nation-building in the 1960s were still quite ignorant of the neighbourhood. They had mostly been trained and educated to look to the metropolitan centres of

11

their respective imperial masters, notably to Britain, Netherlands and France and, in the case of the Philippines, to the United States. Most of them knew much more about those countries than neighbouring countries. This was a major weakness that Dr Goh was very concerned about. Once Singapore became, to the surprise of most people, an independent country with responsibilities for which very few were prepared, its people really had to be very clear where it stood with their neighbours. That was what ISEAS was established for: to be a research institute that would help to explain the new region of Southeast Asia to the people of Singapore.

At the same time, it was clear that Southeast Asia itself was very much a new idea. There was so much to learn about it, so much that we did not know. It was not only Singapore officials who knew little about the region but also those in other countries in Southeast Asia as well. They too were keen to learn about the new states. Thus, other new centres elsewhere soon found it useful to work with ISEAS to expand our knowledge and understanding of one another.

This was the time when the Cold War was spreading and making relations within the region more complicated and tense — the Vietnam War was at its fiercest about the time Singapore became independent. The consequences of the conflict that involved the two superpowers were of great concern to all. It was clear that when the institute started, there had to be a sense of urgency.

I observed this mainly from afar, from Kuala Lumpur and then Canberra. There was growing interest in this region, particularly because of the formation of the Association of Southeast Asian Nations (ASEAN). If I recall correctly, Singapore was not all that clear how that would affect the country and there was uncertainty about the future of such an organization. Nevertheless, the newly independent state needed friendly neighbours and it wisely joined the association.

As the years went by, the situation changed very radically in Indonesia and, less rapidly but nevertheless significantly, on the Indo-China Peninsula as well. When the Vietnam War ended and the future of Cambodia was an open question, the whole region became one with great potential. Not only for ASEAN, at that time seen as mainly the Malay world and Thailand, but also for the region as a whole. It took a while to overcome the ideological concerns of the Cold War years but when the remaining four countries joined ASEAN by the end of the century, this was really an extraordinary development. The region was now becoming a critical part of the security architecture of a larger Asia-Pacific. This made the work of the institute even more important to everyone interested in Southeast Asia.

I see ISEAS at fifty as an institution with still plenty to do. We have a new director taking on this ever-growing responsibility. We wish him all the best.

My second task, again a very pleasurable one, is to chair this meeting for Leonard. Professor Andaya and I have been friends for a long time and I have greatly admired his work for many decades. On behalf of ISEAS, let me say how proud we are to have him launch our anniversary public lecture. Personally, seeing Barbara Andaya sitting in front of us, I cannot resist saying how much I have considered the two of them as one very powerful pair of scholars who have contributed so much to our understanding of the history of the Malay world.

For me, I first met them together when, after their stint at the University of Malaya, they came to the Australian National University, having each done a splendid study of a Malay state, Leonard on Johor and Barbara on Perak. That laid the foundations for the excellent history of Malaysia that they did a few years later that has deservedly become a key text for the country's history. You can see why I have found it difficult ever since to talk about one without thinking of the other; not least also because I have just finished reading the most illuminating history of early modern Southeast Asia that they published in 2015. I am delighted that they are both here to join us to celebrate ISEAS's anniversary.

When I first met Leonard, we talked about his years studying at Cornell University with Professor Oliver Wolters who had had his early career in the Malayan Civil Service and was one of the pioneers in the study of Southeast Asia as a region. Leonard told me how much he learnt from him about the early Malay world of Sri Vijaya and the contemporary states on the mainland that made it possible to see Southeast Asia emerging as a region before the sixteenth century.

Leonard was inspired to go on to study the Malay states. He has not only expanded our knowledge of that extensive Malay world all the way across to eastern Indonesia but also helped us understand how the Malay people came to share a common religion and history. In his major study, *Leaves from the Same Tree*, he provides us with a vivid picture of how the Malay people became open and adaptable, qualities that have enabled them to seek to modernize their societies in their distinct ways. By so doing, he has enabled us to look at the region with fresh eyes. It is now an era when the Malay world is tied up intimately with the mainland and is ready to connect the region's rich and fractured past to an Association that has a great future.

To understand that future, it is essential that we know the region's past, not least about how a group of scholars have redrawn the shape and contours of Southeast Asian history since the end of the Second World War. Leonard has been a major contributor to the study of that scholarly enterprise and very few people are as qualified as Leonard to tell us what happened and how it is still evolving, and thus help us celebrate the Institute's 50th Anniversary.

Developments in the Scholarship of Southeast Asia

Leonard Y. Andaya
Yusof Ishak Professor in the Social Sciences,
National University of Singapore;
Professor of Southeast Asian History,
University of Hawai'i at Manoa

Introduction

It is indeed a great honour to be asked to help celebrate ISEAS – Yusof Ishak Institute's 50th Anniversary by presenting the first of three talks to commemorate this event. Before I begin, I would like to take this opportunity to thank Dean Robbie Goh for his generosity in allowing me to be a part of the Faculty of Arts and Social Sciences at the NUS, and to Professor Itty Abraham and the Department of Southeast Asian Studies for welcoming me into their *ohana* (the "extended family" in Hawai'ian).

In this presentation I will examine some of the developments in the scholarship on Southeast Asia, since I have been part of this enterprise for just a few years longer than the existence of this Institute. I will open with an overview of the evolution of the area studies programmes on Southeast Asia, then proceed to discuss some of the main issues raised by scholars writing about the state of Southeast Asian Studies in the first decade of the twenty-first century, and finally close with a few of my own personal observations on the state of the field.

Evolution of Southeast Asian Studies

Let me begin by looking first at the United States, where the Southeast Asia area studies programme was first developed as an approach. One of the lasting memories that I have of my supervisor at Cornell University, O.W. Wolters (an avid gardener) is his looking over his half-glasses (that he was wont to do to intimidate his graduate students) and warning me: "Do not pick flowers from other people's gardens." Having recently come from the Netherlands, where I had spent a year as a Fulbright student, I thought he was referring to the common practice in Holland called *een avond wandelingetje*, a small evening stroll, where one would pick flowers from public land (but not, I assume, from private property). But this is not what Wolters had in mind; he was instead stressing the importance of doing more original research to add to the corpus of knowledge on Southeast Asia. In 1965 this was a primary concern among American academics working on Southeast Asia, with similar views echoed by other leading Southeast Asian scholars at the time: Harry Benda at Yale (who became the first director of the Institute of Southeast Asian Studies in 1968), John Smail at Wisconsin, and Bob Van Niel in Hawai'i. The goal was to reconstruct the story of the local communities, which had largely been ignored by colonial scholar officials. It was interesting that both Wolters and Benda wanted more research on the "subparts" or the "subregions" of Southeast Asia, where they believed the greatest gap existed.

This development was to take place in a period

of increasing tension in Southeast Asia. By the time I entered graduate school in the fall of 1965, the United States had begun to commit considerable resources and troops to the Vietnam War effort. To develop expertise on Southeast Asia and other regions as a way of countering Communism around the world, the U.S. created the National Defense Foreign Language fellowship to create a pool of people who would be conversant in a critical language. With money pouring into area studies programmes from both government and private agencies, such as the Rockefeller Foundation, Cornell, then the leading institution for the study of Southeast Asia in the U.S., became a veritable academic factory churning out students, theses, and monographs in many disciplines. When my wife Professor Barbara Watson Andaya and I were there in the late 1960s and early 1970s, Wolters had more than fifteen PhD students in history alone, not only from the U.S. but also from Australia, Japan and Southeast Asia. Many of his students came to fill the posts in Southeast Asian history throughout the world. There were similar developments in anthropology, government, linguistics, art history, and rural sociology at Cornell with scholars who made a strong impact on the field. The contemporaries of O.W. Wolters and David Wyatt in history were Lauriston Sharp and Jim Siegel in anthropology; George Kahin, Ruth McVey and Benedict Anderson in government; Frank Golay in economics; John Echols and John Wolf in linguistics; Stan O'Connor in art history; and Randolph Barker in rural sociology. They, like Wolters, were the pioneer scholars in their field and helped shape the nature of Southeast Asian Studies around the world.

The U.S. government's interest in the field of Southeast Asian Studies began to wane after the Americans declared "victory" over North Vietnam in 1972, and much of the funding for the field disappeared with the unification of the two Vietnams in 1975. There followed a downsizing and even closures of some of the Southeast Asian Studies centres, and the flight of American PhDs with now unmarketable skills in Southeast Asian studies to other countries, particularly to Australia and New Zealand. Australia's leading scholars of Southeast Asia at the time — John Legge and Herb Feith, specialists on Indonesia — had both been to Cornell and returned home to develop Southeast Asian studies. Barbara and I were among these academics, going first to Canberra at the Australian National University, where we made the acquaintance of Professor Wang Gungwu and renewed contacts with Anthony Reid, and eventually ended up at the University of Auckland in New Zealand, where we became colleagues with Nicholas Tarling as Southeast Asianists in the history department.

The study of Southeast Asia in the U.S. recovered to a certain extent in the 1980s with the children of refugees and immigrants from Southeast Asia wanting to learn about the history, culture, and languages of their parents. The 1990s were characterized by heated debates on the issue of whether area studies had lost their usefulness and should now give way to the traditional disciplines. Then the 11 September 2001 attack on the twin towers and the Pentagon revived the government's interest in area studies, though now the focus was more on the Middle East and South Asia because of their large Muslim populations.

This then is a brief overview of the evolution of Southeast Asian Studies in the U.S., but there were also other countries that were involved in this enterprise. My knowledge of these other centres is limited, and I had only a few occasions to visit some of them. For this reason, my comments are short and impressionistic.

The Study of Southeast Asia outside the U.S.

Europe and Japan with their colonial pasts have long been interested in the region, while both China and Korea have begun to build a number of different centres, which reflects their growing economic involvement in Southeast Asia. Within Southeast Asia itself, the study of the region has grown with Singapore leading the way with the establishment of the Institute of Southeast Asian Studies in 1968, a brainchild of then Defence Minister, Goh Keng Swee. While there are institutions in Southeast Asia that have developed Southeast Asian Studies programmes, the tendency has been to focus more on the nation-state rather than the region. Nevertheless, such universities as the University of the Philippines, National University of Singapore, the University of Malaya, Chulalongkorn University and Thammasat University were among the earliest and continue to be among the strongest centres in the study of the region.

The proliferation of Southeast Asian Studies around the world has made it impossible to review developments in all the countries. I would therefore like to mention just briefly the direction of Southeast Asian scholarship in Japan because of my own experience there and because of my conversations with Professor Nagatsu Kazufumi of Toyo University, who is now at the Asia Research

Institute at the National University of Singapore for a six-month stint as a Visiting Senior Research Fellow. It may come as a surprise to many that Japan may have more scholars working on Southeast Asia than any other country. In the mid-1980s when we spent eight months at the Kyoto University Center for Southeast Asian Studies, we were told that any publication on Indonesia was assured of sales of at least 10,000 copies at the very outset. I have no recent statistics, but I would expect the interest to have grown rather than waned. In the 1980s and 1990s, Japan was one of the few places where centres of Southeast Asia included scholars from the humanities, the social sciences, and the natural sciences. At the Center for Southeast Asian Studies in Kyoto University, for example, soil scientists and agronomists worked together with geographers, anthropologists and political scientists on specific projects in Southeast Asia. According to Professor Nagatsu, however, this Kyoto model has not survived. Instead, the internationalization of scholarship on Southeast Asia has had an impact on Southeast Asian Studies in Japan, where academics today tend to work individually on projects that reflect global trends. This is a development that can be witnessed elsewhere around the world in Southeast Asian Studies centres.

Concerns in the Study of Southeast Asia

Let me now turn to some of the issues raised by scholars in a series of collections on the state of Southeast Asian Studies. These collections were all published within the first thirteen years of the twenty-first century, most likely inspired by the sense of beginning afresh as we enter into a new era. Among the books that I consulted to compile some of these major concerns were:

- 2000 Itty Abraham, ed., *Weighing the Balance: Southeast Asian Studies Ten Years After* (New York: Social Science Research Council);
- 2003 *Southeast Asian Studies: An Assessment* (Quezon City: UP Press);
- 2003 Anthony Reid, ed., *Southeast Asian Studies: Pacific Perspectives* (Phoenix: University of Arizona Press);
- 2004 David Szanton, ed., *The Politics of Knowledge: Area Studies and the Disciplines* (Los Angeles: UCLA Press);
- 2005 Paul Kratoska, Rembo Raben and Henk Schulte Nordholt, eds., *Locating Southeast Asia: Geographies of Knowledge and Politics of Space* (Singapore: NUS Press);
- 2007 Laurie Sears, ed., *Knowing Southeast Asian Subjects* (Seattle: University of Washington Press);
- 2011 Goh Beng-Lan, ed., *Decentring and Diversifying Southeast Asian Studies: Perspectives from the Region* (Singapore: Institute of Southeast Asian Studies); and
- 2013 Park Seung Woo and Victor T. King, eds., *The Historical Construction of Southeast Asian Studies* (Singapore: Institute of Southeast Asian Studies).

What was missing was any collection on works that had been written in Southeast Asian languages. It would be interesting to see whether concerns expressed among scholars writing in their native tongue were substantially different from those that I have compiled here. This is an important consideration, as I discuss below, and I hope that in the future such collections will be available to provide a more complete assessment of the scholarship on Southeast Asian Studies based on publications in multiple languages.

Here then are some of the important concerns expressed in the above collections:

1. What makes Southeast Asia a region? What is distinctive about it?
2. Where is the Southeast Asian in Southeast Asian Studies?
3. Is there a Southeast Asian approach?
4. Will the dominance of English in the study of Southeast Asia persist and become stronger because of globalization?
5. Is the area studies approach to the study of Southeast Asia still useful, or should it be abandoned for more traditional disciplinary approaches?
6. How should global research and resources on Southeast Asia be made more available to scholars within Southeast Asia?

I would like to deal with the first three concerns first, and then address the others indirectly when I review what I consider to be some new important developments in Southeast Asian Studies.

What Makes Southeast Asia a Region? What Is Distinctive about It?

Some have remarked on the "low self-esteem" of those studying Southeast Asia and of the "fragility" of the concept of Southeast Asia as an area. As Victor King observed, "[T]his preoccupation [with the question of

Southeast Asia as a region] has usually been much more intense when compared with the concerns of regional specialists in other parts of the world."[1] The reasons for this, I believe, are twofold: First, Southeast Asia as a unit of study was a late development, and the artificial nature of its beginnings always raises questions of the region's legitimacy. Second, there has been from early times a tendency to regard Southeast Asia as a hybrid creation from the two major civilizations to its west and east: India and China. Although historians have argued that Southeast Asia was regarded as a distinctive region in China (Nanyang), India (Suvarnabhumi), and the Middle East (Lands below the Winds), the boundaries were never defined. Southeast Asia as a region only began to take shape in the twentieth century. Organizations and institutes, such as the Southeast Asian Games, first known as the Southeast Asian Peninsular Games, which was organized for the first time in 1959 (Burma, Cambodia, Laos, South Vietnam, Thailand, Malaysia, Singapore); ASEAN formed in 1967 (Indonesia, Malaysia, Singapore, the Philippines, Thailand), and the Institute of Southeast Asian Studies (ISEAS) in 1968 were among the first to delineate a membership in "Southeast Asia". The differing composition of those listed as part of "Southeast Asia" in these organizations reflects the lack of consensus on what constituted the region. Southeast Asia as a region is still "a work in progress" with the expansion of ASEAN

---

1. Victor King, "Introduction", in *The Historical Construction of Southeast Asian Studies*, edited by Park Seung Woo and Victor T. King (Singapore: Institute of Southeast Asian Studies, 2013), p. 2.

to ten (and soon to be eleven) nations. The growth of regional organizations through ASEAN and other bodies have resulted in the acceptance today of Southeast Asia as a "legitimate" region. Academically, however, there will always be debates on the artificial divisions created by regional boundaries.

What makes Southeast Asia distinctive as a region is a more difficult question, which I will deal with in a later section.

Where Is the Southeast Asian in Southeast Asian Studies? Is There a Southeast Asian Approach?

This concern is directed at scholarship, collections and workshops where there is an absence or mere token representation of Southeast Asians and the "indigenous" voice, however "indigenous" is defined. The West has continued to set the academic standards in the study of Southeast Asian humanities and social sciences through publications almost wholly in English and through the filters of editors with specific views of what are proper academic subjects to investigate and methodologies to employ. In addition, the Arts and Humanities Citation Index or the Social Science Citation Index determines what is worthy to be recorded and preserved. University administrators in Southeast Asia, as well as in Japan, have contributed to the dominance of Western standards of scholarship by becoming involved in the academic ratings game. To rise in the ranking, universities have basically instructed their academic faculty to demonstrate productivity through publications in English in specifically approved journals that are on the SCOPUS or ISI lists of journals. The result has been the bolstering of English as the language of choice in academic publications, raising issues of the ability of English to translate and transmit accurately concepts that arise from a specific cultural and language context. This is clearly shown in Vince Rafael's *Contracting Colonialism* (1988) and Rey Ileto's *Pasyon* (1979), two international Filipino historians who demonstrate conclusively how Christian ideas preached by Spanish missionaries in the Philippines were comprehended in very different ways within a Tagalog conceptual framework.[2]

A solution recommended in 1996 by the Gulbenkian Commission, composed of scholars from various disciplines and different parts of the world, was more publications in languages besides English.[3] For Southeast Asia, it would be publications mainly in national languages and perhaps even some in regional languages, such as Javanese, which is spoken by some 100 million people. What would be gained in conceptual precision, however, could be lost to a wider academic audience. This has not deterred scholars such as Nidhi Eoseewong in Thailand (trained at Cornell) and Zeus Salazar in the Philippines (trained in Paris), from writing almost solely in their national languages. Many Southeast Asian scholars, however, write in English to satisfy requirements

---

2. Vicente Rafael, *Contracting Colonialism* (Durham: Duke University Press, 1988); Reynaldo Ileto, *Pasyon* (Manila: Ateneo de Manila, 1979).
3. *Open the Social Sciences: Report of the Gulbenkian Commission on the Restructuring of the Social Sciences* (Stanford: Stanford University Press, 1996).

established by university authorities for promotion, but also because they want to engage with the larger academic world and not be regarded as parochial.

Whatever language is used, Southeast Asia has much to offer the academic world not as a place that is distinctive from any other region, but as a site for some notable features. Among these are ecological and human diversity; the cross-fertilization of indigenous belief systems and external religions; the existence of strong oral and written traditions and their interplay in literature and the arts; the role of water (seas, rivers, brackish water) in the lives of Southeast Asians; and the communities that are associated with the region's extensive seas, forests and hills. These are subjects that require more research in whatever language in order to provide the bases for comparative studies with other regions of the world.

Despite the fear expressed by some of the danger of homogenization through globalization and the dominance of the English language, this has not eventuated. Instead, in Southeast Asia and elsewhere around the world, there has been a process of "glocalization", where the global is adapted to local conditions and made part of the local. Paradoxically, increasing globalization has contributed to the expansion of what it means to be local. This can be seen in the development in ethnomusicology, pop art, music, literature, and the visual and performing arts — all inspired by global trends but localized to form exciting novel creations that help raise the local to a new level.

I would now like to turn to what I consider to be important developments in Southeast Asian Studies. The field has expanded so dramatically that it is no longer possible for one individual from one discipline to do justice to the many developments in the field. Please view the following comments, therefore, as a personal perspective from a historian of Southeast Asia.

My View of New Developments and Directions in Southeast Asian Studies
The ICT Revolution

One of the most important developments in scholarship in general has been the Information and Communications Technology (ICT), which has contributed to an explosion of information through a proliferation of websites and databases. With the increasing accessibility to information and the speed in which it can occur, the issue of sharing of knowledge is no longer as much of a problem for Southeast Asians as in the past. However, there is still a wide gap in accessibility to this new technology both because of the differing levels of technological infrastructure and because much of the information is in English. Yet among the educated population and the academic institutions, much more is now being shared than would have been the case even just a few years ago.

As a result of this ICT revolution, the research agenda is no longer the sole domain of tertiary institutions, international bodies or governments. Through academic listservs, social media and specialized websites, civil society organizations (CSOs) have been able to create virtual communities within Southeast Asia and beyond and hence influence the research agenda. The result has been publications on indigenous rights, LGBTQ issues, the environment, and feminist perspectives on Islam as advocated by Sisters in Islam in Malaysia.

Networking is far more possible today leading to a "transnational model", where the origin and location of scholars and scholarship are no longer as significant as in the past. Mobility of personnel has always been a feature of academia, and with many institutions around the world willing to hire scholars who teach in English, academics working on Southeast Asia are now found in institutions in all parts of the world. Moreover, scholarship has become more internationalized. Today, scholars from around the world studying Southeast Asia have access to English and other Western languages, along with Southeast Asian ones, and thus able to keep pace with other scholarship on the region. Ease of travel to Southeast Asia, accessibility to English and hence to an international academic community, growing number of scholarships and short-term visiting positions within Southeast Asia itself have all contributed to the internationalization of the field. The growth of study abroad programmes and short summer programmes for the study of Southeast Asian languages or for field studies in archaeology have broadened the knowledge and perspective of students from the region and elsewhere. Students and scholars studying Southeast Asia today are being challenged to look beyond the nation-state towards more regional and inter-regional issues.

The ICT revolution has also extended the boundaries of area studies to incorporate diasporas, international labour, and refugees as legitimate areas of scholarly inquiry. With ICT, diaspora communities can continue to be linked to their home country while being equally rooted in their host society. This new type of community has made diaspora studies an important part of area studies. The worldwide phenomenon of temporary migrant labour from Southeast Asia, particularly from the Philippines and Indonesia, working in Asia, Europe, the Americas, and the Middle East, and the significant impact of their remittances to their home countries make international labour another subject of significance in Southeast Asian Studies. Finally, wars and political upheavals have contributed to the flood of refugees moving within and beyond the region, making it necessary to move beyond Southeast Asia to study this phenomenon.

While the ICT revolution has been transformative, it has not been invulnerable to government censorship, with some countries even employing thousands of "cyber warriors" to patrol the Internet for "subversive" noises. Another weapon used by authorities is the firewall to prevent unauthorized Internet users from accessing private networks connected to the Internet. We have already seen this at work in the most authoritarian governments within Southeast Asia, where scholars presenting academic papers at international conferences have been subject to persecution and prosecution by their governments. In face of this development, it is necessary for a protocol to be introduced to assure the safety of Internet users and to guarantee the freedom of information. This may be a forlorn hope in face of ASEAN's policy of non-interference in the domestic affairs of its members. Yet, if scholars in Southeast Asia can use their networks around the world to highlight abuses, perhaps they could influence ASEAN to be more assertive in safeguarding this important freedom.

An "Open System" in Academic Inquiry

Another development, which is directly linked to the area

studies versus disciplines debate, is the call for an "open system", where the boundaries of scholarship are not determined by artificial borders — whether constructed by governments, international organizations, or academic bodies — but by the subject matter. It is not a new idea but had been raised earlier by the geographers Martin Lewis and Kären Wigen in their *Myth of Continents* (1997),[4] which argued for the need to focus on ecological spaces wherever they occurred, rather than being confined to nation-state (or even area studies) boundaries. Goh Beng-Lan in her introduction to the edited volume, *Decentring and Diversifying Southeast Asian Studies* (ISEAS, 2011), has also suggested new globally oriented approaches such as the seas, zomia, subregions, and, I would add, "transitional regions (between eastern Indonesia and Oceania, or between Myanmar and India and Bangladesh, or between southern China and northern mainland Southeast Asia)". Such units of investigation occur within the region but are global concerns that transcend area studies boundaries.

Thematic studies are already being done in the Asia Research Institute (a unit of the Faculty of Arts and Social Sciences in the National University of Singapore) in focus groups called "clusters".[5] Southeast Asianists have been able to learn and to contribute through useful comparisons

---

4. Martin Lewis and Kären Wigen, *The Myth of Continents* (Berkeley: University of California Press, 1997).
5. Some clusters have ended, but the current ones in 2018 included Asian Migration, Asian Urbanisms, Changing Family in Asia, Cultural Studies in Asia, Religion and Globalization, and Science, Technology and Society.

across regions in Asia. Encouraged by such comparative studies and by global academic trends, Southeast Asianists have begun to conduct innovative studies on the environment, pop culture and social movements (such as new religions). The multidisciplinary approach in many of these works on Southeast Asia reflects what Clifford Geertz has called the "blurring of genres", where scholars have often found it necessary to rely on more than one traditional discipline to understand fully what was being studied. For those of us who work on Southeast Asia as a region, the area studies/discipline debate is of limited relevance. Any respectable study of the region will perforce employ multiple disciplines because of the nature of the subject and the availability of sources.

Global comparisons are also becoming an essential part of Southeast Asian Studies. This trend is not threatening but encouraging a deeper knowledge of the region in order to bring Southeast Asia into the global picture. There continues to be, therefore, a need for research on cross-regional issues as well as national ones, to provide the basis for regional and global comparisons. The internationalization of scholarship and the common use of an academic lingua franca (English) have created the opportunities for Southeast Asianists to engage in such comparative studies and to flourish in this new academic environment.

Presentism in the Study of Southeast Asia

A persistent feature in Southeast Asian Studies has been the emphasis on topics that are of current interest and thus considered "relevant". This presentist bias has been encouraged by governmental bodies and academic institutions that require results to justify ongoing funding. Students are aware of this bias and tend therefore to study subjects that would be saleable in the job market. Such subjects as literature, art history, languages, premodern history, archaeology and paleography are suffering from lack of interest not only among students but also in traditional disciplinary departments within universities. One of the casualties of the Orientalist critique has been the debasing of textual studies of Southeast Asian manuscripts. Yet it is these manuscripts that offer an indigenous voice and contribute to Southeast Asia's identity. It is time to encourage more textual studies by scholars trained in both philology and literary criticism.

The ISEAS – Yusof Ishak Institute and Southeast Asian Studies

Let me conclude by paying tribute to ISEAS – Yusof Ishak Institute, where the focus on modern issues has not resulted in the neglect of the past. In 1966 Dr Goh Keng Swee acknowledged the need for well-rounded expertise in policy-making, and so he encouraged research in contemporary political and economic issues while "not losing sight of the importance of history as a guide not only to the past but also to the future".[6] It was this vision that led to the creation of the ISEAS – Yusof Ishak Institute. While issues of the environment, security, terrorism, politics and international relations will continue to be its driving concerns, the presence of

---

6. Lee Kim Chew, *ISEAS: Studying Southeast Asia* (Singapore: ISEAS – Yusof Ishak Institute, 2015), pp. 157, 170.

the Nalanda-Sriwijaya Centre (created in 2008) with its current emphases on archaeology, art history, premodern history and maritime archaeology have partially fulfilled Dr Goh's earlier hopes.

The Institute is also fortunate in being able to draw on the deep and extensive expertise on Southeast Asia that is available at the National University of Singapore, particularly in the Faculty of Arts and Social Sciences with the Asia Research Institute and the Departments of Southeast Asian Studies and Malay Studies. More and closer collaboration among these institutions and departments can only strengthen the study of Southeast Asia.

The Institute continues to be a dynamic entity. Its impressive publication record, its role as convenor and facilitator of regional conferences and cooperation, and its promotion of scholarship on the region through short-term grants have made it one of the most influential bodies in Southeast Asia. Let us hope that it will continue to function as a major centre for the study of Southeast Asia for at least another fifty years.

50th Anniversary Public Lecture

by

Prime Minister Lee Hsien Loong

on

13 March 2018
4.30 p.m. to 6.00 p.m.
Orchard Hotel, Singapore

Opening Remarks

Professor Wang Gungwu
Chairman, ISEAS Board of Trustees

Prime Minister, Distinguished guests, Friends and colleagues of ISEAS – Yusof Ishak Institute, Ladies and Gentlemen

It is a privilege to have Prime Minister Lee Hsien Loong deliver his lecture at ISEAS' 50th Anniversary today. I must say there is a nice symmetry to the occasion because exactly twenty-five years ago ISEAS had the pleasure of hosting Prime Minister Lee (then Deputy Prime Minister) as our Guest of Honour at our 25th Anniversary in 1993.

I should also add that it was ten years ago that we had the honour of hosting Minister Mentor (MM) Lee Kuan Yew for the Institute's 40th Anniversary in 2008. MM Lee graced a very stimulating dialogue that ranged from domestic politics to global geostrategic trends. And it was this combination of domestic politics in the region and the geostrategic trends that saw the need for the establishment of an institute like ISEAS fifty years ago.

ISEAS was set up in 1968 as the brainchild of Dr Goh Keng Swee at a time when the region was trying to build new nation-states and also seeking to form a regional organization like the Association of Southeast Asian Nations (ASEAN), both at the same time. Dr Goh saw that it was essential to understand what was happening to Southeast Asia and what the unfolding trends would mean for Singapore.

Dr Goh visited several renowned research centres and think-tanks when he was thinking about ISEAS. They included Chatham House in the United Kingdom, the Council on Foreign Relations, the Rand Corporation in the United States, and also a number of universities with strong Southeast Asian programmes like Yale, Cornell and Berkeley.

In his discussions with these institutions, Dr Goh quickly realized that the soon-to-be-formed ISEAS had to be something very different, a special institution that served Singapore's unique needs. For example, he noted that:

> The Rand-type of think factory can only be created in a continental superpower and is not within our horizon of possibilities. Nevertheless we can draw a few lessons from Rand's working and recruiting methods and its insistence on high-quality personnel. Chatham House and the Council on Foreign Relations are again unsuitable because of their total concern with contemporary events. What we need is research into matters not of immediate value in policy-making but which are necessary to the development of well-rounded expertise.

Dr Goh's pragmatism and clarity of mission have been instrumental in shaping ISEAS' research agenda. We are interested in both contemporary developments with clear policy implications as well as the less obvious, less eye-catching trends, which may have implications further down the road.

Over the years, ISEAS has been the beneficiary of strong support from the government, enabling it to develop the way it has done today. This support has been given while dealing with us at arm's length to preserve our academic and research independence. I believe that this approach has enabled the Institute's scholars to make valuable contributions to what the world now knows about the region's developments, which has become extraordinarily complex during the past half-century.

By following Dr Goh's pragmatism, our research focus and capability have evolved with a changing external political, regional and international environment. To keep up with this greater research responsibilities, we have established new units to take on a wider range of research areas. This has enabled us to study and share our findings and analyses on regional and international politics as well as on economic and social developments with the wider academic and policy community.

We have worked with government agencies, business organizations, NGOs, as well as international organizations and other research institutes both within and beyond the region, and in this way, enhance the value of our research work.

As we progress into the next decade, we can be sure that there will be momentous changes in our region, within neighbouring countries, and between those countries as well. We also know that new trends such as anti-globalization, nationalism generally, as well as increased major power rivalry, all these together may imperil our stability and economic success and undermine ASEAN's centrality as an organization. These are possibilities that we have to bear in mind. My colleagues are aware of these fresh challenges and are determined to study these changes and trends and contribute, as much as we can, to understanding these issues more deeply.

Mr Prime Minister, with your support and that of our many collaborators, we are optimistic that our research will continue to be relevant and impactful. Once again, on behalf of the ISEAS – Yusof Ishak Institute, thank you for joining us today as our guest for the special occasion as ISEAS gears itself up to continue its work in the years to come.

With that, I have come to the end of my opening remarks.

It is my great pleasure now to invite Mr Lee Hsien Loong, Prime Minister of Singapore, to deliver the 50th Anniversary lecture for ISEAS – Yusof Ishak Institute.

Mr Prime Minister, please.

ISEAS 50th Anniversary Lecture

Lee Hsien Loong
Prime Minister of Singapore

Prof Wang Gungwu, Chairman of ISEAS – Yusof Ishak Institute, Mr Choi Shing Kwok, Director of ISEAS – Yusof Ishak Institute, distinguished guests, ladies and gentlemen. I am very happy to be here to celebrate ISEAS – Yusof Ishak Institute's 50th Anniversary. As Professor Wang just told you, I was privileged also to celebrate your silver anniversary in 1993, twenty-five years ago. I am glad to be back again, a quarter century later, to mark this further milestone.

ISEAS was one of the first research institutes that the government set up after Singapore became independent. In fact, Dr Goh Keng Swee proposed this idea to Cabinet in 1966, just one year into our nationhood. Subsequently, ISEAS was established in 1968.

Why did our founding fathers think of setting up ISEAS, amidst all the pressing economic and social issues they faced? We had high unemployment, a stagnant economy, race relations were still tense after the two race riots when we were in Malaysia. We needed to build houses and schools, to clear slums and create jobs, and gradually foster a sense of nationhood. Yet amidst all these priorities, the founders stepped back from their day-to-day concerns, reflected on Singapore's strategic situation, and decided to invest resources and talent into building a research institution to study Southeast Asia.

Why did they do this? Having lived through momentous upheavals, they understood instinctively how closely our fate was intertwined with the region's. The war was a not very ancient living memory. Southeast Asia was still a troubled and unstable region. Singapore had just separated from Malaysia. *Konfrontasi* was barely over. President Suharto had only recently taken charge and restored order in Indonesia.

The region was on the frontlines of the Cold War. Communist forces had made advances in Indochina, the Vietnam War was hotting up. Thailand, Malaysia and Singapore, all faced communist insurgencies. The insurgencies were encouraged and supported by China, which was then in the throes of the Cultural Revolution.

Our founding fathers were acutely conscious that to survive in such a difficult environment, a small and newly independent country needed to acquire a deep understanding of the region. Because small countries do not shape world events, events shape us. In Dr Goh's words, Singapore had to acquire a "delicacy of perception" of the affairs in the region so that we could foresee difficulties and opportunities and prepare in advance to address them.

But this "delicacy of perception" was then seriously lacking in Singapore. In the Cabinet paper proposing the setting up of ISEAS, Dr Goh pointed out that "we know more about Melbourne than we know Medan, more about the English Channel than the Sunda Straits"!

Dr Goh also believed this expertise had to be developed outside the government. The government's policy and intelligence officers would be too bogged down by immediate, day-to-day concerns to look at regional issues from a long-term, detached perspective. By creating an institute that operated separately from the government, we could house eminent academics and researchers to develop deep knowledge of the subject matter. They could then provide the government with independent insights, looking through alternative lenses, on the same issues which government officials had been working on.

ISEAS was thus created as an autonomous organization by an Act of Parliament in 1968. Over the last fifty years, ISEAS has established itself as a respected research institute on Southeast Asian affairs. This achievement is the work of generations of chairmen, directors and distinguished fellows. They include Professor Wang Gungwu, Professor Kernial Singh Sandhu, Dr Sharon Siddique, Professor Chan Heng Chee, Mr Kesavapany, Mr Tan Chin Tiong and Mr Choi Shing Kwok, several of whom are here today.

I would like to especially mention Professor Wang Gungwu and Professor Kernial Singh Sandhu. Professor Wang is ISEAS' longest-serving chairman, having been chairman and served with distinction since 2002. However, his association with ISEAS goes back even further. In fact, he was one of the candidates considered to be ISEAS' founding director in 1968. But at the time, he had other commitments. Nevertheless, he served ISEAS in varied capacities over the decades before becoming chairman. He was a member of ISEAS' first Regional Advisory Council, which has since become the International Advisory Council. ISEAS has benefitted from Prof Wang's advice, knowledge and dedication to academia and guidance. Therefore, it is befitting that ISEAS has honoured Prof Wang with a permanent gallery in the ISEAS Library displaying his books, private papers and photos.

Prof Kernial — the late Prof Kernial — was ISEAS' longest-serving director. He served for twenty years from 1972 to 1992. Prof Kernial laid lasting foundations for ISEAS during his tenure. He established the annual ISEAS Roundtable which attracted government officials, scholars and businessmen from around the world to exchange views on Southeast Asia. He launched several publishing initiatives notably the *Southeast Asian Affairs* journal. Today, ISEAS is the region's leading research centre. It has produced more than 2,000 books and journals, the largest scholarly publisher of research on Southeast Asia and Asia Pacific.

ISEAS marked another significant milestone three years ago when we renamed it the ISEAS – Yusof Ishak Institute. It was a tribute to Encik Yusof Ishak, Singapore's first President, who had dedicated his life to modernization and education, and whose values were congruent with ISEAS' own. It was also a reminder of ISEAS' long history and strategic mission.

Southeast Asia and ASEAN

Like ISEAS, Southeast Asia has come a long way in the last fifty years. In 1967, the year before ISEAS was formed, the leaders of Indonesia, Malaysia, the Philippines, Singapore and Thailand took a leap of faith and formed the Association of Southeast Asian Nations (ASEAN). The original five members were later joined by Brunei and, later still, Vietnam, Laos, Myanmar and Cambodia, bringing ASEAN to ten member states.

ASEAN's original objective was political. The five founding members wanted a regional platform for dialogue and co-operation. They wanted to put old suspicions and hostilities behind them, to work through new problems and conflicts peacefully and constructively. To foster a stable environment within which each country could concentrate on its own nation-building. This objective was achieved.

One major test for ASEAN was dealing with the Vietnam–Cambodia conflict from the late 1970s onwards. ASEAN then consisted of six members, the original five plus Brunei. The members had different perspectives on the matter. For example, Thailand was a frontline state, with a border with Cambodia, while the Philippines and Indonesia were one step removed. It was a considerable diplomatic achievement that the ASEAN members came to a common understanding and adopted a unified ASEAN stand. ASEAN rejected a *fait accompli* achieved by force of arms. It insisted on the international rule of law, the inviolability of international borders, and the legitimacy of national governments. It advocated its position forcefully and effectively at many international fora, including the United Nations and the Non-Aligned Movement. It helped bring about the eventual political settlement and security of Southeast Asia for all ten of ASEAN's present member countries who at that time were not on the same side. This experience strengthened ASEAN and provided members the basis to broaden their collaboration beyond security issues. The next focus was economic co-operation.

Initially this had not been a high priority. The focus had been politics. When ASEAN began exploring economic co-operation in the early 1980s, the members found ourselves in very different economic positions. Singapore had an open economy and was strongly pro-market and pro-trade. But other ASEAN economies were less outwardly oriented, and varied in their readiness to liberalize their economies and to promote free trade. It therefore took several years for economic co-operation to build up momentum. I remember participating in the discussions. I was then in the Ministry of Trade and Industry and we, for the first time, were talking about a free trade area amongst the ASEAN counties. I well remember at one of the early discussions, one of my counterparts saying, in all seriousness and sincerity to the group, we should not put up proposals to our leaders, which our leaders would have to say no to. In other words, he did not feel that ASEAN was ready politically to embark on an initiative as bold as a Free Trade Agreement (FTA). But over time as ASEAN economies developed, perspectives shifted. By 1992, we were able to launch the ASEAN Free Trade Area (AFTA), a milestone in our economic co-operation. We have come far since then.

Today, the ASEAN Economic Community (AEC) is a prime example of how ASEAN is larger than the sum of its parts. Together, the ten diverse countries make up a dynamic and attractive economic group. It has a growing population of 630 million, which is more than 100 times Singapore's population. Of which, 60 per cent are under 35 years old. By 2030, we expect more than 60 per cent of the population to join the middle class. ASEAN will be fourth largest single market in the world, after the United States, China, and the European Union (EU).

From the broader strategic perspective, ASEAN has also strengthened its members' standing in the world. It has enhanced our collective voice on the international stage. It has put ASEAN at the centre of the regional architecture. It has enabled us to engage major countries like the U.S., China, India, and Japan, and key organizations through ASEAN-centric platforms. It is a long list, I will just name a few and spare you the alphabet soup. ASEAN+1 meetings, ASEAN+3, the East Asia Summit, the ASEAN Regional Forum, and the ASEAN Defence Ministers' Meeting Plus.

Today, the ASEAN Community has three pillars: economic, political-security, and socio-cultural. We will continue to pursue closer integration under this framework and progressively strengthen the ASEAN Community. However, ASEAN will not become an ASEAN Union, on the model of the EU. It is less ambitious than the EU in terms of scope, membership and integration. ASEAN does not aim to have an ASEAN Parliament, an ASEAN Court of Justice, an ASEAN currency, or an ASEAN Central Bank, not even in the very long term. ASEAN is too diverse to aim for a European-style union. Our countries have different histories and cultures, diverse political and economic systems, contrasting views of the world. Where our interests align, we work together. Where we are not ready to co-operate, we put matters aside for the time being, to take up perhaps later when conditions are riper.

In recognition of this diversity, ASEAN works by consensus. This decision-making process can be slow and unwieldy. We can only move when all member states agree. Sometimes if there is no agreement, we may not move at all. But this arrangement has, on the whole, served us well because it requires member states to recognize and consider one another's national interests, irrespective of the size of the member states.

One area where ASEAN countries do not have a unified stance and for fundamental reasons, is our strategic outlooks. A clear instance of the impact of this, and how ASEAN members can find common ground despite our differences, is the South China Sea dispute, or issue. Not all ASEAN members are claimant states. Even among the four claimant states — Vietnam, Malaysia, Brunei, the Philippines — there are different concerns, attitudes and nuances. ASEAN has to recognize this diversity. But we are still able to find common ground because all member states share certain common interests on this issue. Ensuring ASEAN's relevance, upholding the international rule of law, securing regional peace and stability, and maintaining freedom of navigation and overflight in the South China Sea. Therefore, we are able to agree to take progressive and constructive steps to manage the disputes and overlapping claims, for example, by concluding a Code of Conduct in the South China Sea, on which ASEAN has commenced negotiations with China.

Therefore, while this consensus-building process is laborious, it has its uses and merits. Member states find it meaningful to work together to seek common ground. They do not think of opting out from or leaving the group because their sovereignty or national interests have been suppressed or undermined. And ASEAN, once it has arrived at a decision, does not change its position lightly. External partners therefore see value in deepening their engagement of the region and ASEAN.

Looking Ahead

Looking ahead, ASEAN must continue working hard to remain an effective and central player in the region. The twenty-first century is a very different world from the 1960s, when ISEAS and ASEAN were formed. The Cold War is long over. Southeast Asia today is largely peaceful and stable but there will always be hotspots and difficult issues to deal with from time to time. We also have to adjust to a strategic balance which is shifting both globally and in the region. New powers are growing in strength and influence, especially China and India. Individual ASEAN countries must adapt to the new and changing strategic landscape. Countries have to take into account the policies and interests of new powers, while maintaining their traditional political and economic ties.

There will be new opportunities. China has put forth concrete, major initiatives such as the Belt and Road Initiative and the Asian Infrastructure Investment Bank that will benefit the region. India, too, is cultivating its relations with ASEAN and pursuing a more activist foreign policy beyond the subcontinent. Individual countries stand to benefit, and so potentially will ASEAN as a whole. At the same time, the ASEAN grouping has to get used to new internal dynamics, as each member feels the influence of the different powers to different degrees. We must accept the reality of these tidal pulls without allowing them to lead to fault lines forming within the ASEAN group.

All ASEAN countries want to maintain and develop their ties with the U.S., even as the U.S. is intensely reviewing its trade and foreign policies. The U.S. is still the region's security anchor and the world's largest economy. We recognize that the political mood in the U.S. has changed. The Trump administration is rethinking America's international role, and how the U.S. should advance its interests and influence in the world, and it is rethinking radically. However, the U.S. has clearly affirmed its determination to stay engaged in Asia. Countries hope that it will continue to play an active role, particularly in Southeast Asia.

In this shifting environment, it is important that ASEAN works actively to maintain its centrality and relevance. ASEAN centrality is crucial and yet ASEAN has no automatic right to be the centre of the regional architecture. There is nothing to prevent other groupings or regional co-operation projects from being launched. Some will compete with ASEAN, others will contribute in complementary ways to regional co-operation and stability. The Belt and Road Initiative and the Free and Open Indo-Pacific are two examples. Amidst this Darwinian process, ASEAN members must come together to maintain ASEAN's relevance and cohesion. Only thus, can ASEAN remain at the heart of the regional architecture, and a valuable partner and interlocutor for the major powers. What should ASEAN members, and ASEAN as a group, do to keep ASEAN relevant and cohesive?

First, it is important that each member state supports and promotes the ASEAN project. Each ASEAN member has its own domestic issues and politics to handle. Governing a country internally is already an all-consuming affair. But ASEAN governments need to look beyond their domestic concerns, put emphasis on ASEAN, invest political capital in the ASEAN project, and make a conscious effort to think regionally, not just nationally. Only with this commitment by member states can we deepen our partnership and make progress in ASEAN.

ASEAN countries have given their support to the grouping, gradually but progressively, over the years. We supported one another through difficult times such as the Asian Financial Crisis, the SARS outbreak and various natural disasters. Now we are co-operating in new areas including counter-terrorism, climate change, e-commerce and cybersecurity.

We have also adopted the ASEAN Community Vision 2025 to develop new blueprints for the ASEAN Political-Security Community, ASEAN Economic Community and ASEAN Socio-Cultural Community. We have laid out progressive steps, such as deepening transport connectivity and co-operation against transnational crime, to strengthen the ASEAN Community.

As the ASEAN Chair this year, Singapore will do its best to take the group forward through our Chairmanship themes of "resilience" and "innovation". We will initiate projects to strengthen our collective resilience against common threats such as terrorism, cybercrime and climate change. We will help ASEAN economies to innovate and to use technology, to build a more dynamic and connected community. One key project in this field is to establish an ASEAN Smart Cities Network, to create attractive places in all our countries to live, work and play.

Externally, ASEAN needs to deepen its web of co-operation with major partners. We are working on the Regional Comprehensive Economic Partnership (RCEP), which comprises ASEAN and our six FTA partners. When established, it will be the world's largest trading bloc, covering about a third of the world's gross domestic product (GDP). We are also working with the EU on the ASEAN-EU Comprehensive Air Transport Agreement (CATA). This will be the first substantive aviation arrangement between two major trading blocs. The RCEP and ASEAN-EU CATA will bring tangible benefits to our peoples and our partners. But they involve significant trade-offs and compromises. The decisions will not be easy, because so many parties are involved, and especially given growing mood of nationalism and protectionism in many countries. But I hope governments will take a long-term approach, assess their enlightened self-interests, and make bold decisions which will improve our people's lives.

For half a century, ASEAN governments have taken such an approach and brought ASEAN to where it is today. This is a remarkable achievement, far exceeding what the founding leaders of ASEAN had imagined. The decades of intense interactions have helped to deepen mutual understanding amongst members and to socialize us to think regionally, and not just nationally. This should equip ASEAN countries to cope with the more challenging environment that we are now in and to build further on what ASEAN has already achieved.

Conclusion

Southeast Asia and ASEAN, therefore, will remain a big

part of Singapore's mindshare and our foreign policy. Therefore, Singapore needs to maintain a "delicacy of perceptions". To come back to Dr Goh Keng Swee's phrase, towards developments in our region, we need this "delicacy of perceptions" not just among Ministers and government officials, but also our intelligentsia, our financial and business community, our media and Singaporeans of many professions who need to know our region in order to work, to do business, or just to know how to get along with our neighbours and partners. Therefore, ISEAS continues to play an important role, enriching our collective knowledge of the region. I hope it will, in this process, enhance mutual understanding among our ASEAN partners too.

I am confident that ISEAS will rise to the challenge and continue to do remarkable work so that ASEAN will truly become "One Vision, One Identity, One Community". I wish ISEAS every success in its next fifty years. Thank you very much.

50th Anniversary Public Lecture

by

Professor Wang Gungwu

on

3 October 2018
3.00 p.m. to 4.30 p.m.
Orchard Hotel, Singapore

Opening Remarks

Professor Barbara Andaya
Professor of Asian Studies, University of Hawai'i

Ladies and Gentlemen, Friends and Colleagues,

We are here today to listen to Professor Wang Gungwu's thoughts on the prospects and potentialities of a world before "Southeast Asia", and also to honour a scholar who has been a giant in the field of Asian Studies for more than two generations. Some of you will remember that earlier this year, in March, Professor Wang stood at this podium to introduce Prime Minister Lee Hsien Loong, and it was thus somewhat daunting when I was asked to follow in his footsteps and introduce his own presentation, the third in a series of lectures celebrating the 50th Anniversary of the ISEAS – Yusof Ishak Institute. I was especially humbled as I thought of the eminent people who have spoken or written about Professor Wang's achievements as an intellectual and a public spokesperson on so many topics related to the history and present condition of the Asian region. Indeed, I was at a loss as to what I could add to the many tributes that have celebrated his career — his service to the University of Malaya between 1957 and 1968, his time as Professor and later Director of the Research School of Pacific Studies at the Australian National University (1968–86), as vice-chancellor at the University of Hong Kong (1986–95), and since then in Singapore where he has been Director of the East Asia Institute and University Professor at the

National University of Singapore, the highest honour NUS can bestow. We are all very aware of the global recognition Professor Wang has received — honorary doctorates from some of the world's most prestigious universities, and international awards recognizing his long history of service to scholarship and to the public more generally. However, on this occasion we remember especially his long association with the ISEAS – Yusof Ishak Institute, his unwavering support for the concept of a research centre devoted to regional studies, his valuable donations to the library and his leadership as Chairman of the Board of Trustees.

This commitment to an institute where the voices of Southeast Asians would be heard and where Southeast Asian debates could find a forum stretches back deep into the past, and it is here perhaps that I can make my own intervention. When I entered graduate school in 1966, one of the first works I was assigned to read was Professor Wang's study of Nanhai trade, submitted as an MA thesis to the University of Malaya in 1954 and published four years later. In covering ten centuries of early Chinese commerce with the southern seas, Professor Wang — then a very young scholar — stressed the importance of local perspectives and of viewing the Nanhai trade not just as exchange of goods, but as the basis for "a more lasting intercourse" of ideas. While the theme of the relationship between China and Southeast Asia has continued throughout Professor Wang's career, *The Nanhai Trade* also registered his interest in the notion of a more inclusive region that was not fettered by the political borders that developed in later times. As a student of premodern Southeast Asia it was thus a formative personal encounter when I arrived at the Australian National University (ANU) in 1975, where Professor Wang had just taken up an appointment and was working to raise the profile of Southeast Asia in Australia more generally. He had been a key person behind the formation of the Asian Studies Association of Australia the previous year and later served as its President. In today's world, conferences abound, but in the 1970s this was not the case. I still recall Professor Wang's involvement in my first international conference, one dealing with "perceptions of the past" in Southeast Asia, and his telling comment that "perceiving the past is not enough; it is how the past is used that matters". Perhaps what lingers most in my mind about my Canberra days are the frequent gatherings at the Wang home, where the generosity and hospitality of Professor and Mrs Wang contributed to a welcoming and relaxed environment where students and faculty at all levels could talk and socialize. This is perhaps the appropriate place for me to express on behalf of everybody here our affection, admiration and thanks for the support, intellectual and practical, that Mrs Wang — Margaret — has provided to Professor Wang during their marriage of sixty-three years. The kindness she and Professor Wang showed to young scholars, especially women, was something for which I will always be personally grateful. At a time when gender relations may seem fraught, it is heart-warming to read that Professor Wang has himself gone on record as saying that human progress "cannot be separated" from the position of women.

During my time in Canberra I was also privileged to see Professor Wang as a consummate administrator, invariably respectful of opposing points of view, which must surely reflect his upbringing from parents steeped in the courtesies and traditions of China, but also his early exposure to a range of different personal experiences and different cultures. As a young man growing up in Ipoh he lived through turbulent times — the Japanese occupation of Malaya and then the contentious period of decolonization and nation-building, which he witnessed not only in Malaya and Singapore but also during the two years he spent as a student in Nanjing during the nationalist–communist struggle. We are fortunate that many of his views have been laid out in his published interviews and most recently, in the account of his early years, published by NUS Press and launched just last evening. Beautifully weaving his own memories around those of his mother, he has been able to convey a sense of the unsettling experiences of identity-creation for many individuals for whom (to use the title of this book), "home is not here". Yet over time Professor Wang's very love of learning and his thirst for reading led to the realization that through his own experiences and the rich multicultural environment that literature generated, he was "learning in different worlds" and that he could find a home in many places.

Given this global movement — from Ipoh to Nanjing, to Singapore and London, to Canberra and Hong Kong — it is hardly surprising that over the years Professor Wang has often been described as a "bridge" between cultures. One could say that this remains a hallmark of his contribution to the study of Asia — he is not merely a great scholar of the past and an insightful commentator on the present: he is an interpreter who has helped his audiences understand the history and culture of others, but simultaneously aids them in their own self-realization and self-reflection. His bridge-building capacity is evident not merely in his ability to connect histories of different societies and cultures, but in the inspiration he has given to academic interaction through interdisciplinary discussions — between history and international relations, for instance, or history and archaeology, and between the new field of migration studies and the history of overseas Chinese. In fulfilling his overlapping roles of a teacher and commentator, scholar and public intellectual, Professor Wang's greatest skill is the ability to truly listen; when one talks to him one always feels one has his undivided attention. Moreover, it is not merely individuals who receive his attention. Easily adapting to new environments, he talks and writes about subjects that are contextually grounded but also raises more general questions — one thinks, for example, of his study of the Chinese Australian Bill Liu, written after he took up his position in Canberra, the numerous publications in Chinese that appeared while he was in Hong Kong, and in the twenty years since his return to Singapore, an amazing output of publications and lectures, as well as his leadership role on the boards of various institution, especially the East Asia Institute and of course the ISEAS – Yusof Ishak Institute.

As a final comment, I would like to express my remarks personally to both Professor and Mrs Wang: I just want to say how very privileged we all are to see this example of a true partnership, and to say a heartfelt "thank you" to both of you for all your years of unstinting service. Professor Wang, we are all eager to hear your presentation today, entitled "Before Southeast Asia: Passages and Terrains", and I invite you now to come to the podium.

Before Southeast Asia: Passages and Terrains

Professor Wang Gungwu
Chairman, ISEAS Board of Trustees

Introduction

When the term "Southeast Asia" was first used, many at that time were surprised and intrigued by the idea that this part of the world had been recognized as a region. After all, the "region" is a geographic and spatial concept; and Southeast Asia was, in reality, a very diverse set of lands. In using the phrase "passages and terrains" in my title, I will try to capture the tremendous range of connections (passages) and landscapes (terrains) that make up this region. Indeed, this range makes it challenging to imagine Southeast Asia as a region. On one hand, we see all the highlands and lowlands from the various great rivers of mainland Southeast Asia. On the other, the Malay archipelago with thousands of islands which were recognized as some kind of geographical unit but never quite able to draw themselves together into a political unit. To understand Southeast Asia today, we have to reimagine what it meant.

Furthermore, why did it take us so long to identify the region of Southeast Asia? This is where historians come into the picture. For though geographers would work it out spatially, historians had long thought that there was not that much to tell about this region. It certainly took dozens of historians to get the ball rolling and to ask fundamental questions about the region as a whole. What is it all about? What is this region? Why was it not recognized as a region in the past? The last question was the most intriguing one. Immediately historians, particularly those outside the region, had their imaginations stirred by the concept of Southeast Asia as a region. Initially they had little to go on because one of the reasons why Southeast Asia was not earlier recognized as a region was because there was not a great deal of literature (books, official records, documents) on it. So at the very beginning, historians had to work with linguists, archaeologists, anthropologists who were equally curious about this thing called "Southeast Asia" and what it could possibly mean.

In the midst of all that, the historian was quick to ask the question: Who are the people? What is the capacity of these people to do something and to make something of this tremendous variety of terrains and passages? I can think of three main periods which would be useful for us in understanding how the concept of Southeast Asia has evolved: the periods before the sixteenth century; the sixteenth to eighteenth century; and the eighteenth to twentieth century, including the 1960s to the present as the crucial years for the formation of ASEAN and nation-building in the region.

Before the Sixteenth Century: Diverse and Open

Prior to the sixteenth century the people living in these passages and terrains were as diverse as the physical environment they found themselves in, if not more so. They were scattered in the valleys on the mainland or around the islands that constituted the Malay archipelago. They were fragmented into all sorts of little units, none of them really capable of coming together to sustain a major political unit for long. So this question of capacity was immediately in the minds of historians: Why were they not able to act earlier to bring other people together to establish a powerful political entity? In the end, I suppose it all boils down to the fact that capacity depends on the ability to produce reserves and create wealth, and then to have some kind of organization to sustain that wealth and to protect and defend it. The larger the organization, the greater the capacity to draw these fragmented places together. That must be the underlying basis. So why were these people unable to do that?

I believe that it was not a matter of being unable to organize but a matter of intention. After all, there were efforts to organize themselves into smaller units. However, there was no intention to organize themselves into large, singular and complex political configurations. This was because deep in their culture from the very beginning, and the historians and archaeologists can confirm it, these people, especially those on the Malay archipelago, had a certain openness about influences and relationships, which enabled them to move around effortlessly. They were a tremendously mobile people and the waters made it easier to connect, reach out, and build subtle, complex relationships without setting out some huge bureaucratic system to run it. They never needed it and did not seem to care whether they had it or not.

Of course, there were some exceptions. One can point to that of the Khmer rulers who over several centuries built the huge complex that we know as Angkor and whose armed forces dominated an extended area on both sides of the Mekong. But they left no viable state system behind and their exceptional successes were lost to the jungle. The other was on the island of Java where some states did have organizational capacity. Here we also have evidence of their openness to new ideas and institutions. The people in Java were remarkably open to a wide variety of ideas coming from the West and at that time the "West" meant India. Ideas of the state, religion, art, architecture and literature came from India. The locals responded to these ideas, combined them with some of their own ideas and faiths and drew them together into a set of values which they have more or less preserved for a thousand years afterwards. As a result, there is evidence of some semblance of a bureaucratic state in early Java.

But elsewhere in the archipelago, there were little signs of such a state. They did not need it. They functioned in their own little ways — in what Barbara Andaya has also referred to as "local genius"; that is, the local way of responding to external complexities and influences, the ability to pick and choose what they wanted, and making the most of it for their own purposes. They were content with the diverse and fragmented areas, all interlocking in one way or another. And they thrived during that period.

I underlined the fact that they were very open. This is a strong residual characteristic from ancient times in this part of the world. This openness was brought about by the sea from the very beginning with people migrating to the islands from the mainland, whether from southern China or southwestern China. The openness also came from migration down the river system from southwest China or even from Tibet into mainland Southeast Asia. This openness was not only to ideas but also to the trade of goods and commodities which provided them the surpluses and capacity to build healthy societies.

Underlying this openness was a certain self-confidence and assurance that they could always pick and choose what they needed and not feel inferior or insecure about it. This kind of self-confidence — in a way it is self-respect — allowed them to be contented with the kind of autonomy each of those units had. It was a kind of confidence to deal with one another without fear, without needing to set up some big bureaucratic system. I thought that was quite a strong characteristic that Oliver Wolters and other historians would later agree to compare with the "mandala" complexes in India — the loose relationship between various autonomous units — rather than the bureaucratic systems that established powerful centralized states elsewhere.

The Sixteenth to Eighteenth Century: Awareness from Beyond

Things changed around the sixteenth century that marked the beginning of some awareness of Southeast Asia as a region. But this awareness really came from the outside. External powers began to find it convenient to treat the coastal areas of Southeast Asia as areas that had much in common. These powers found the Indian Ocean too vast to control because of its extensive waterway from East

Africa to the Bay of Bengal. In contrast the South China Sea was more manageable. It was relatively small and already well used as the main route of communication among trading entities whether on the mainland or on the islands, resulting in numerous connections.

We now have enough evidence, especially archaeological evidence, to show the extent to which all these units were in touch with one another. Exchanges of goods and ideas were taking place all the time. For example, the Chams of Champa were very mobile and the coastal lands they controlled served as a major passage for trade between the region and China. They were also very mobile over the waters connecting the Malay peninsula with Java and Sumatra.

Even land-bound people such as the Funanese or the Khmer from the Angkor empire also had sea connections, though not as extensive as those on the Malay archipelago and the Cham people from the mainland. Conversely, the people in the region were receiving people from the north. There were always people moving down from the north but this was particularly so after the thirteenth and fourteenth centuries, probably because of the Mongol expansion from Central Asia into China, notably to southwest and southern China. The power of the Mongols represented a completely new force. Most historians agree that there was no force as consistently powerful in Eurasia as the Mongols over 200 years. At sea, there is the example of the Tamil kingdom of the Cholas that intervened and changed the course of the trading relations of Sriwijaya empire but that was for a only brief period without any lasting consequences.

The Mongols, on the other hand, were tremendously powerful. It invaded China, took over the Chinese capacity for maritime power, and used it against Java as well as against Vietnam and Champa along the coast. On land, they moved into southwest China, destroyed the kingdom of Dali in Yunnan, and threatened Burma as well as Vietnam. They went further at sea and tried to attack Japan. They failed but the force they unleashed was something quite new. The Mongols sustained their power for some 150–200 years and that was carried forward by the Chinese from the beginning of the Ming dynasty for another 100 years or so. It marked the beginning of a borderland between the Yuan and the Ming empires and the overland frontiers of Vietnam and Burma. That border was not yet firm but it was the beginning of a separation of two regions. The Ming, however, did not pursue that power in the south. In the end they turned away from the sea and concentrated on continental defences. Their mandarins lost interest in this part of the world.

After the sixteenth century we see the coming of the Europeans. That was new. These early Europeans did not come in sizeable numbers. They were neither overwhelming nor dominating. They were effective with their powerful ships that made a difference in trading patterns and controlled many regional harbours. The Portuguese set up a chain of ports which became the model for two East India companies in the next 200 years.

Meanwhile in Europe, and for reasons completely baffling to us in Asia, the Catholic Church determined how the world should be divided. We had the Spaniards coming across the Pacific from the other side to take the Philippines, creating a completely new corner of Southeast

Asia which was locked into a Pacific future rather than with the rest of the region. And indeed the Philippines looked away from the region for the next 300 years, and has remained somewhat of an outlier ever since. Again this was a beginning of our imagination of Southeast Asia. For with the Philippines turning to the Pacific on one side, and with the Chinese Ming border overland on the other side, we begin to see the shape of Southeast Asia.

One does not see a border between the Western part of Southeast Asia and the rest of the Indian Ocean countries. This was because the Indian Ocean was simply too huge and thus served as a natural border-zone that nobody had to think about. But the European ships came freely back and forth. The Portuguese, followed by the Dutch and the British, made the Indian Ocean into a vast lake of their own. They controlled it for the next 200 years.

The Eighteenth to Twentieth Century: Colonial Powers, New Borders and WWII

The eighteenth century was another turning point for Southeast Asia. Developments in Europe had led to greater technological advancements. The Industrial Revolution and emerging forms of capitalism provided the basis for modernity. And yet while European modernity began to shape Southeast Asia, I do not think anybody was conscious of this shaping at that time. Interestingly, looking at the geographical terms used in the nineteenth century, there was still no clear reference to the region that we now identify as Southeast Asia. There were terms like "Malaisie" which denoted the Malay archipelago. There were terms like "Indochine" or "Indochina" which referred to mainland Southeast Asia between China and India. So there were all kinds of names being suggested but none caught the imagination. This was partly because the European powers coming into this part of the world were creating a new type of diversity and fragmentation. They were marking out a new set of borders. Certainly in the Malay archipelago, new borders were being created by the Dutch on the one side and the British on the other. By this time the Portuguese had been edged out of the main areas.

The series of major wars in Europe, driven by new weaponry and powerful instruments of domination, also had their impact. These wars were no longer about religion or between Catholic and Protestant states. They started with the French Revolution, produced Napoleon, and began to profoundly change the map of Europe. The Napoleonic wars also changed the map of Southeast Asia because they influenced the British–Dutch relationship. Further change occurred because the British had defeated the French at sea in the Indian Ocean, thus allowing the British navy to eliminate the French as the challenger to its dominance. And it was the complete domination of the Indian Ocean that made it possible for the British to move into India so confidently and take over the whole of the subcontinent.

That naval dominance could lead to bold ventures into the interior of the mainland was a new phenomenon. Before this, coastal power was defined as the control of ports, linking up commercial interests, and safeguarding shipping routes. But to be strong and confident enough at sea in order to take over land territory was new. It had happened overland before with Mongols and the

Moguls in India, but never by sea. The Dutch and the French were limited in their success with a bit of Ceylon and a few islands in the Indian Ocean, respectively; but they were mainly confined to port control without ever going too far in.

With regards to Southeast Asia, the Dutch moved into Java in the nineteenth century, though on a small scale compared to the British moving into India, but this was the first time such movement occurred in the region. These colonial powers proceeded to look at Burma, putting pressure on Thailand, moving into the Malay peninsula, moving again into Vietnam, first in southern Vietnam and steadily in the nineteenth century into its interior reaching the border of southwest China. From these movements you can see the shaping of Southeast Asia. With so few land troops backed by strong naval forces, these colonial powers dared to move into hostile valleys whether up the Menam or the Irrawaddy or along the coast of Vietnam, and going further inland into Cambodia or northern Tonkin. With the British so caught up in India that they could not do it themselves, the French came back and went into Indochina.

This was the shaping of the region by colonial states. And I refer not to mere colonial ports but colonial states; each possessing a bureaucratic structure derived from Europe. They were modern and sophisticated, introducing new laws and systems of governance, new ways of thinking about how rulers behaved and how people should be ruled. And as with all new states, new borders were drawn up.

This brings us to another turning point — the twentieth century. Two developments were crucial here.

First was the way Southeast Asian mainland states were divided between France and Britain. This took most of the nineteenth century leaving half of the mainland in the hands of the French and another half more or less in the hands of the British. The Thais skilfully manoeuvred between the two in order to survive but recognized that they were economically dominated by both the French and the British. And both European powers never failed to remind the Thais of this fact.

By the twentieth century the borders had firmed up. The Thai borders were drawn: between Thailand and Laos, and between Thailand and Cambodia although they quarrelled with each other for a long time afterwards; between Burma and Thailand, drawn by the British following the first and second Burmese wars. The third Burmese War reached up to Yunnan and settled that border with China. Vietnam's border with China had been settled by the fifteenth century when the last Ming's attempt to invade Vietnam failed. In fact, this border was more or less the same one that was drawn up between China and Vietnam in the tenth century. Nevertheless, it was firmed up and is the oldest Asian border that I know of. Firming up the Laotian and Burmese borders was the final act of the French and the British together with China.

It was also around this time when the Japanese had learned from the West: how to build a strong navy, how to manufacture the things that the West manufactured, and how to be an economic power tied to the free market economy and capitalist system. They were such quick learners that they also picked up other Western habits. Japan's first colonial act was to move into Taiwan.

Some people say that it started with the Ryukyus, but certainly taking Taiwan after 1895 was the major step into this region. Because whether we think about it or not, Taiwan was really on the edge of Southeast Asia. It is not and has never been part of Southeast Asia but it was the entry point by sea into Southeast Asia from the north. The Chinese did not need it to do so because China had Guangdong, Guangxi and Fujian. But for the Japanese, to get into Southeast Asia, they would need Taiwan as an opening. It was significant that the Japanese in Taiwan and the Americans in the Philippines created a new front that now began to shape Southeast Asia on the maritime side.

Again, it is interesting that we never had any question about the western side of Southeast Asia. It is significant that the island of Sumatra and its separation from the other places on the other side of the Bay of Bengal never came into question. The distances between ports in the large expanse of the Indian Ocean seemed enough to provide a natural boundary.

The region's defining moment in the twentieth century was the Japanese invasion of Southeast Asia in 1941. The British and Dutch strategic thinkers, as well as those of the French and the Americans, knew that the Japanese had ambitions. They of course did not expect it to happen the way it did with the attack on Pearl Harbour. The Japanese invasion of Southeast Asia was the first recognition of a region that was separate from China and that could be connected with India. The Japanese tried to prove this by using Burma as the base to attack India, drawing forces from the Indian National Army to help them support India's independence from

Britain. The agenda was to drive Westerners out of Asia and form the "Greater East Asia Co-Prosperity Sphere" that was meant to unite all Asians against the West with Japan as their leader. That Southeast Asia might not have been all of the Nanyo — the southern ocean region — because Nanyo to the Japanese also included Oceania and Australia, but the part that they could conquer was certainly recognized by the Japanese as a region. And they took all of it in a matter of months.

Bear in mind that at the peak of Japan's power in Southeast Asia in 1942, every coast of the South China Sea was under Japanese control. The French in Indochina was under Vichy and had no say in what was happening off their coasts. Thailand was more or less a puppet. The rest of Southeast Asia was directly under Japanese rule, from the Philippines, northern Borneo, whole of Indonesia, to the Malay peninsula, and of course to the northern edges of Burma.

By that definition, the South China Sea was effectively a Japanese lake. Tokyo controlled the whole of it. This reminds us of the centrality of the South China Sea in the definition of Southeast Asia and why, to this day, it is the South China Sea that arouses our attention whenever we talk about Southeast Asia. But it is important to recognize that the South China Sea has always included China because the northern coast of the South China Sea was China. South China Sea is not a Southeast Asian sea. It has always been a sea shared between the Malay archipelago, the mainland and southern China.

While the Japanese invasion gave definition to the region, so too the British expulsion of Japan. The British created the "Southeast Asia Command" as a site of military theatre, from which we get the term "Southeast Asia" today. It was a strategic name with added significance because Mountbatten was appointed to head the Southeast Asian Command first in India and then moved to Ceylon. These two things — the Japanese invasion and the response to the invasion — were instrumental in creating the region of Southeast Asia as we know it.

By 1950s, geography books and history books on "Southeast Asia" began to come out. Universities in London, Australia and the United States took up the challenge of defining Southeast Asia in terms of the long history of the region, how it became that region, why it deserves to be separated and recognized for its own identity, personality and character. And all this interest and impetus began largely from 1941 to 1945 — four critical years when the shaping came to a head. Finally, Southeast Asia became real in the eyes of more and more people.

The 1960s to the Present: Evolving ASEAN and Nation-Building

And we have recognized Southeast Asia ever since. The Association of Southeast Asian Nations (ASEAN) is simply a product of this discourse. We also recognized that the original ASEAN-5 (Indonesia, Malaysia, Philippines, Singapore, and Thailand) was a product of the Cold War because Southeast Asia was divided and the Vietnam War was raging. The fear of a communist takeover of the region, including the domino theory, led many to believe a bulwark was needed and ASEAN-5, some would say, was an extraordinary and unexpected result of the

Gestapu coup in Indonesia. The fact that Sukarno was overthrown and Suharto came into power within the two years of 1965–67 enabled ASEAN to come about. And I think it would be true to say that without Indonesia under Suharto, there would not be an ASEAN.

In sum, the years from 1963 to 1965 and from 1965 to 1967 reshaped Southeast Asia again. It gave ASEAN-5 a semi-regional role in a region divided by the Cold War, but the role was not meaningful until the late 1970s following the end of the Vietnam War and the Vietnamese invasion of Cambodia. ASEAN during the first few years was not going anywhere. The organization was extremely uncertain about what it could do except for its members to try to get to know one another better. In 1968, the Singapore government, just three years after independence, established the Institute of Southeast Asian Studies (ISEAS) in recognition of the fact that the newly formed city-state could not hope to flourish without understanding the region. Indeed, in ISEAS's early years, studying Southeast Asian meant studying the ASEAN-5 countries.

Along the way there were several events which impacted Southeast Asia in their own way. The Vietnam War came to an end, Mao Zedong passed on, the rise of Deng Xiaoping saw a new China that identified with the maritime market economy and this led to rapid changes in its policies. Of these the most impactful event was perhaps the end of the Cold War in 1991. This left us with one superpower — the United States — that was more or less in charge of the world.

The 1990s were eventful for ASEAN too. ASEAN-5 became ASEAN-10 with the encouragement of the United

States. At that time, China was awakening but had not yet risen. For the first time ASEAN became a truly regional body for Southeast Asia. With ten member states, it could be confidently said that there was a "Southeast Asia" that was operating through ASEAN; even to add that this was capable of developing into a self-assured and self-respecting region which has a future. But of course there were new challenges, chief among them globalization and intensive nation-building.

The market economy had created borderless economies around the world, opening up national communities to external flows and influences. This coincided with the fact that for the fifty years since the 1950s, every country in ASEAN had embarked on a journey of nation-building and national identity. The result was a tension between the national and the global. Another profound process that many Southeast Asian countries were undergoing was the transition from colonial to modern nation-state. The diversity, fragmentation, and local genius that were deeply entrenched in the past were now being reshaped as modern nation-states, each with a new identity built upon the borders of the colonial states.

After all, the different colonial states left different heritages. The French in the three Indochina states and the Dutch in Indonesia left distinctive elements behind although nationalist revolutionaries replaced their respective administrations. The British left different constitutional structures in Malaysia and Singapore. The Thais of course have maintained their own traditions. Burma (now Myanmar) had generated a way of defining itself starkly from the rest. I do not think any ASEAN country has been totally comfortable with their transition from colonial to modern nation-state. Nevertheless, this transition has been relatively successful. It has demanded great sensitivity and tremendous care from ASEAN leaders in managing differences within their own countries as well as those with their neighbours. In fact there were two new processes that ASEAN itself was undergoing at the same time.

On one hand a newly created ASEAN gave Southeast Asia a fresh sense of regionalism and community. For once, diverse communities could indulge in a sense of collectivity. On the other, there were strenuous efforts by member states to build nations that would be separate and clearly distinct from one another. These processes were sometimes contradictory; and certainly, in some cases, slowed down the possibility of a regional identity that people strove for. This tension between a modern concept of a nation-state and the idea of a region will remain with us for some time.

ASEAN is definitely a work-in-progress. The officials involved in the ASEAN experiment have done extremely well to have kept it together all this time. It has demanded traits such as political sensitivity, the willingness to compromise, and the give-and-take mindset that ultimately leads to consensual agreement. While critics have described them as obstacles to the development of ASEAN unity, they are not new traits. They are deeply rooted in the region's history and should not be dismissed or taken lightly. They will be with us for a long time, and the region has to take them into account in their engagements with one another. I am happy to say that almost all the leaders in the region are very sensitive to this reality.

For the last fifty years, and this is particularly true for the first five ASEAN member states, the first two or three generations of officials have developed a very good understanding of each other. The four member states after the 1990s are also producing this kind of officialdom and their officials are working together closely. This is encouraging but it has to be recognized as work-in-progress. Meanwhile there are people saying with some urgency that ASEAN must be united. ASEAN must be one and must talk with one voice. Every one of these calls is correct and understandable. It is in the region's interest to be united and to speak with one voice so that the big neighbours from beyond would respect the region and give it a hearing whenever it speaks up. And yet, this unity cannot be rushed because of the many differences within.

Furthermore, I would hasten to add that calls for unity must be met with discernment. Calls for unity from within ASEAN is one thing. ASEAN leaders understand the challenges and the need to operate within complex relationships. However, calls for unity from the outside are, ironically, sometimes louder than those from within. I am always astonished by the number of outsiders who want ASEAN to be united. Sometimes I wonder why. The reasons are varied, each with a different motive behind it. Ultimately, calls for ASEAN unity from the outside are so that the region would unite on their side against the other side. As parties outside the region engage in rivalry, each party would want ASEAN to be united for them against their rivals. This is perfectly understandable. And so ASEAN leaders have to constantly weigh all this. After all, the internal calls for unity are based on very different principles from the external calls for unity.

Conclusion

All this brings me to my last point — the fundamental openness of this region. As mentioned at the start of the lecture, people in this region had the capacity to take in new ideas, pick and choose what suited them, adapt them for their purposes, and make them their own. They eventually internalized such ideas as part of their own culture and value systems. The capacity to do this over the last 2,000 years is amazing.

And I believe it is still there. It is something that is common to Southeast Asia. Southeast Asian do not adhere to a single order or follow a single set of norms and rules. Instead, their diversity and fragmentation have resulted in different ways of approaching different problems. But they possess the confidence and assurance of knowing what they want, and they all seek a kind of autonomy within a larger unity. This autonomy within a unity is, to me, something that will continue in Southeast Asia. The desire for both autonomy and regional unity will exist for a long time and should not be regarded as a weakness. It may even be a strength because this autonomy and local genius could make the region more self-confident.

It is true that there are voices around the world calling for protectionism in one way or the other. However, while multilateralism and globalization may have had their ups and downs, they are, in my view, irreversible. The region should embrace this openness as it always have and pick and choose new ideas, adapt them, and internalize them to strengthen the ASEAN body. This openness should be encouraged, not feared. I believe that the leaders of ASEAN member countries should, given the historical roots of their openness, face the threats and dangers that come with openness, overcome and learn from them, and then create new opportunities for themselves. This is something that ASEAN countries must reintegrate into their way of thinking to make this region stronger.

www.ingramcontent.com/pod-product-compliance
Lightning Source LLC
Chambersburg PA
CBHW060347100426
42812CB00003B/1158